The Good Dog

Walker Jean Mills

Walker J Mills

ISBN 978-1-64003-344-3 (Paperback)
ISBN 978-1-64003-345-0 (Hardcover)
ISBN 978-1-64003-346-7 (Digital)

Covenant Books, Inc.
11661 Hwy 707
Murrells Inlet, SC 29576
www.covenantbooks.com

Dedicated to all the *good dogs* both on earth and in heaven.

The vet entered the waiting room and told Daisy, "You can see your dog, Charlie, now."

Daisy burst through the door, put her head on Charlie's neck, and whispered, "You are a good dog. You do good things…

You welcome me home.

You help me do my chores.

You listen to my problems.

You play with me when no one else will.

You always put a smile on someone's face.

You take care of my bumps and bruises.

And you wipe away my tears when I am sad."

Daisy then whispered to her dog Charlie, "I love you, Charlie. You are a good dog. And like you, I want to do good things. I want to…

Wipe away a friend's tears when they are sad.

Welcome my parents home.

Help with the chores.

Listen to other people's problems.

Play with others when no one else will.

Put a smile on someone's face.

And I *most* want to take care of my dog's bumps and bruises."

After kissing Charlie's stitches, Daisy scratched Charlie's head and hugged him, beaming, "Charlie, you are a good dog. You do good things. Let's go home and do good things together!"

34

Be kind and compassionate to one another, forgiving each other, just as in Christ God forgave you. - Ephesians 4:32. New International Version

About the Author

Walker grew up in Birmingham, Alabama and works and plays in the Rocky Mountains. She received her bachelor's degree from Birmingham Southern College and master's degree from Colorado State University. She currently works as an occupational therapist in the Colorado public school systems, helping children experience success in their meaningful childhood activities. She does have a dog named Charlie. She loves him very much.

CPSIA information can be obtained
at www.ICGtesting.com
Printed in the USA
BVHW020540081019
560431BV00008B/451/P